the PIANO MAGIC of
FLOYD CRAMER
Gospel Classics

ISBN 978-0-692-57516-1

Copyright © Jason Coleman Music
P.O. Box 1211, Goodlettsville, TN 37070

For all works contained herein,
Unauthorized copying, arranging, adapting, recording or public performance is an infringement of copyright.
Infringers are liable under the law.

www.JasonColemanMusic.com

WHAT IS A SLIP NOTE?

Floyd Cramer described his signature *slip note* style as "hitting the wrong note first, then slipping up to the right note" – an intentional mistake followed by an immediate correction. It's a similar sound to a steel guitar or a fiddle sliding from one note to the next.

In addition to that quick note change in the melody, Floyd would also play a harmony note one interval above the melody. In Southern Gospel quartet music (which he grew up listening to and playing), it's like singing a high tenor harmony part above the lead part.

A *slip note* is different from a *grace note,* though. While a grace note typically comes BEFORE the beat so that the correct note falls ON the beat, a slip note falls ON the beat and the correct note comes just AFTER the beat.

For example, here is the opening line of Floyd's most famous song, *Last Date:*

The melody is found in the middle notes of each chord. To play the slip note in the first chord, you would play the F-G-C interval with your thumb, index finger, and little finger, then immediately "slip" from the G (the "mistake") to the A (the "correction"), with your middle finger while still holding the F and C with your thumb and little finger.

In these arrangements, the slip notes are most frequently written as sixteenth notes for ease of reading, but the actual length of the slip note is sometimes a bit quicker. Listen closely to the accompanying Play-Along CD – as well as your favorite Floyd Cramer albums – to get a feel for exactly how the songs are intended to be played.

ABOUT THE PLAY-ALONG CD . . .

The CD that accompanies this songbook features two recordings of each song in the book – the odd-numbered tracks are *demonstration* versions featuring the piano and band together, while the even-numbered tracks are *"play-along"* versions with the piano part removed so that YOU can play piano along with the band.

DEMO

PLAY-
ALONG

The CD track numbers for the demonstration and play-along versions of each song are indicated at the start of each arrangement.

BLESSED ASSURANCE

Words by FANNY J. CROSBY
Music by PHOEBE PALMER KNAPP

Gently, tenderly

Arranged by Jason Coleman
Copyright © 2015 Jason Coleman Music
International Copyright Secured   All Rights Reserved

4

Amazing Grace

Arranged by Jason Coleman
Copyright © 2015 Jason Coleman Music
International Copyright Secured   All Rights Reserved

JUST A LITTLE TALK WITH JESUS

Words and Music by
CLEAVANT DERRICKS

Copyright © 1937 The Derricks Legacy (BMI) (adm. at CapitolCMGPublishing.com)
All Rights Reserved   Used by Permission

His Eye is On the Sparrow

Words by CIVILLA D. MARTIN
Music by CHARLES H. GABRIEL

Arranged by Jason Coleman
Copyright © 2015 Jason Coleman Music
International Copyright Secured   All Rights Reserved

IN THE GARDEN

Words and Music by
C. AUSTIN MILES

Arranged by Jason Coleman
Copyright © 2015 Jason Coleman Music
International Copyright Secured   All Rights Reserved

PEACE IN THE VALLEY

Words and Music by
THOMAS A. DORSEY

Soulfully

There Will Be Peace In The Valley For Me
Copyright © 1939 (Renewed) WARNER-TAMERLANE PUBLISHING CORP.
This arrangement Copyright © 2015 WARNER-TAMERLANE PUBLISHING CORP.
All Rights Reserved   Used by Permission
Reprinted by Permission of Hal Leonard Corporation

MORNING HAS BROKEN

Words by ELEANOR FARJEON
Music by CAT STEVENS

Copyright © 1972 Cat Music Ltd. and BMG Rights Management (UK) Ltd., a BMG Chrysalis company
Copyright Renewed
This arrangement Copyright © 2015 Cat Music Ltd. and BMG Rights Management (UK) Ltd., a BMG Chrysalis company
All Rights Reserved   Used by Permission
Reprinted by Permission of Hal Leonard Corporation

THE OLD RUGGED CROSS

Words and Music by
REV. GEORGE BENNARD

Arranged by Jason Coleman
Copyright © 2015 Jason Coleman Music
International Copyright Secured   All Rights Reserved

ABOUT THE ARRANGER — JASON COLEMAN

Jason Floyd Coleman was only 12 years old when his grandfather, piano legend Floyd Cramer, passed away in 1997, but the relationship they shared formed the foundation upon which Jason has built his own career in music.

At age 17, Jason made his Grand Ole Opry debut, and two years later, he was given the honor of playing for the Medallion Ceremony recognizing Floyd's induction into the Country Music Hall of Fame. In 2006, Jason graduated from Belmont University in his hometown of Nashville, Tennessee with a degree in music business.

Since then, he has spent his career in the studio and on stage, producing a collection of his own albums and performing across the country in concerts that pay tribute to his grandfather's enduring legacy and signature "slip note" piano style.

Jason lives in Hendersonville, Tennessee with his wife, Natalie.

MORE MUSIC FROM JASON . . .

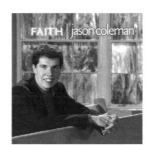

The Piano Magic of Floyd Cramer
Songbook of country and pop classics

Also available – beautiful albums featuring Jason on the piano!
Listen and purchase on Jason's website and on iTunes.

Find out more about Jason's music online at
www.JasonColemanMusic.com

JasonColemanMusic @JasonPlaysPiano